# Comptroller's Handbook          A-OREO

## Safety and Soundness

| Capital Adequacy (C) | Asset Quality (A) | Management (M) | Earnings (E) | Liquidity (L) | Sensitivity to Market Risk (S) | Other Activities (O) |
|---|---|---|---|---|---|---|

# Other Real Estate Owned

September 2013

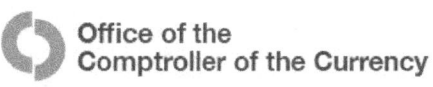

**Office of the Comptroller of the Currency**

Washington, DC 20219

# Contents

# Introduction

The Office of the Comptroller of the Currency's (OCC) *Comptroller's Handbook* booklet, "Other Real Estate Owned," provides guidance for bank examiners and bankers on the acquisition, management, disposition, and accounting of other real estate owned (OREO) held by institutions regulated by the OCC. Institutions include national banks and federal savings associations (FSA), referred to collectively in this booklet as banks, except when it is necessary to distinguish between the two.

National banks and FSAs are subject to some differing regulations. FSAs are subject to regulation regarding the holding period for OREO but have no regulations regarding the disposition of OREO or additional expenditures on OREO; these issues are addressed by policy. By comparison, national banks are subject to regulations regarding the OREO holding period, OREO disposition, and additional expenditures on OREO. The regulations governing appraisals and evaluations for national banks and FSAs are the same.

OREO is real estate, including capitalized and operating leases, that is

- acquired through any means in full or partial satisfaction of a debt previously contracted.
- a former banking facility including a property that was acquired for future expansion but for which banking use is no longer contemplated.

For regulatory reporting purposes, OREO also includes

- equity holdings, such as limited liability companies, that indirectly represent real estate acquired through foreclosure or by deed in lieu of foreclosure.
- real estate collateral securing a loan when the bank has obtained physical possession of the collateral, regardless of whether formal proceedings have been instituted against the borrower.
- foreclosed real estate sold under contract and accounted for under the deposit accounting method in accordance with the Financial Accounting Standards Board's Accounting Standards Codification (ASC) subtopic 360-20.

While this booklet focuses on foreclosed real property, the acquisition accounting and reporting guidance described in this booklet is applicable to other types of foreclosed (repossessed) property, such as consumer and commercial goods, financial instruments, and intangible assets.[1] For reporting purposes, as with real property, other foreclosed assets include loans where a bank has received physical possession of a borrower's assets, regardless of whether formal proceedings take place.

---

[1] Guidance for other repossessed property can be found in the "Installment Loan" booklet of the *Comptroller's Handbook* and the Federal Financial Institutions Examination Council (FFIEC) call report instructions.

# Authority to Hold

12 USC 29 permits a national bank to hold certain types of real estate, including OREO. 12 CFR 34, "Real Estate Lending and Appraisals," subpart E-OREO, implements this statute and contains additional requirements relating to the OREO holding period, disposition, appraisals, and additional expenditures and notifications. OREO may be held directly or indirectly through equity ownership in an entity formed to hold the real estate. See appendix A for additional information.

Included in 12 CFR 34 is a section that says a national bank should normally use real estate acquired for future bank expansion within five years. After holding such real estate for one year, the bank must state, by resolution of the board of directors or an appropriately authorized bank official or subcommittee of the board, definite plans for the real estate's use. Such resolution or other official action must be available for inspection by national bank examiners. If at any time during the five-year period such property is no longer being considered for banking use, the property must be transferred to OREO. The five-year holding period for property acquired for future bank expansion also applies to FSAs.

An FSA's salvage powers are derived from 12 CFR 160.30, "General Lending and Investment Powers," and permit the acquisition, holding, and operation of OREO and the expenditure of additional funds in regard to OREO. These powers provide FSAs with inherent or implied authority to take any necessary steps—including investing additional funds and salvaging an investment—provided the steps taken are an integral part of a reasonable and bona fide salvage plan and do not contravene specific legal prohibitions. (Note: The lending limit is not considered to be a specific legal prohibition within the meaning of the salvage powers doctrine.)

# Risks Associated With OREO

From a supervisory perspective, risk is the potential that events, expected or unexpected, will have an adverse effect on a bank's earnings, capital, or franchise or enterprise value. The OCC has defined eight categories of risk for bank supervision purposes: credit, interest rate, liquidity, price, operational, compliance, strategic, and reputation. These categories are not mutually exclusive. Any product or service may expose a bank to multiple risks. Risks also may be interdependent and may be positively or negatively correlated. Examiners should be aware of this interdependence and assess the effect in a consistent and inclusive manner. Refer to the "Bank Supervision Process" booklet of the *Comptroller's Handbook* for an expanded discussion of banking risks and their definitions.

While price risk is the primary risk presented by OREO, liquidity, operational, compliance, and reputation risks may also be present. These risks are often interdependent, and each should be considered when assessing the quantity of risk OREO presents to a bank.

Real estate price declines during the holding period can reduce the proceeds that may be realized upon a property's disposal. Economic trends that may have played a role in the bank's acquisition of the property as OREO could continue, and values may be further diminished by the sale of properties by other banks or distressed borrowers. It may be difficult to obtain accurate valuations in markets experiencing volatile sales prices or in markets dominated by distressed sales. A bank may find it challenging to realize the market value of a property because of potential purchasers' perceptions that the bank may be anxious to dispose of it.

Real estate is by its nature illiquid. High levels of OREO and ineffective disposal strategies negatively affect a bank's liquidity.

Operating policies and procedures for OREO can pose operational risk that may result in reduced property revenues and excessive expenses, uninsured casualty losses, inadequate or ineffective marketing and sales efforts, collateral deterioration, unrecognized losses, and lower recoveries.

A bank assumes substantial compliance risk when it acquires OREO. A bank must comply with relevant laws and regulations, beginning with the foreclosure process and continuing through ultimate disposition of the property. A bank has legal responsibilities with regard to owning, operating, and maintaining OREO and may be held liable for damages to other parties. Foreclosure activities involving residential properties, in particular, can pose significant compliance risk.

The acquisition of OREO can negatively impact a bank's reputation in several ways. A bank's reputation may suffer when it manages OREO in an imprudent manner, owns an unpopular or deteriorated property, or employs foreclosure management practices that are inconsistent with OCC guidance, local or state laws, or federal regulations. These practices can create negative public opinion, which in turn may impair a bank's competitiveness by affecting its ability to establish new relationships or maintain existing relationships.

## Risk Management

The OCC expects each bank to identify, measure, monitor, and control risk by implementing an effective risk management system appropriate for its size and the complexity of its operations. When examiners assess the effectiveness of a bank's risk management system, they consider the bank's policies, processes, personnel, and control systems. Refer to the "Bank Supervision Process" booklet of the *Comptroller's Handbook* for an expanded discussion of risk management.

## Policies and Procedures

A bank should have appropriate policies and procedures in place to govern the acquisition, holding, and disposition of OREO. A bank's policies and procedures must be consistent with financial reporting requirements and applicable laws and regulations, and should comply with supervisory guidance issued by the federal banking agencies.

Acquiring title to properties—either for the bank or as servicer for a third-party mortgagee—results in new or expanded risks. The bank should be sure it has identified these risks and has policies and procedures for monitoring and controlling them. The "Managing Foreclosed Properties" section of this booklet describes the obligations and risks that bank management and the board of directors should consider in developing the bank's OREO policies and procedures as owners of foreclosed properties. Appendix B, "Guidance on Potential Issues With Foreclosed Residential Properties as Servicer or Trustee," describes the obligations and risks that should be considered when servicing for others. While the focus of the guidance for foreclosed properties is primarily on residential properties, many of the principles also apply to commercial properties.

# Holding Period

There are restrictions on how long a national bank or an FSA can hold OREO. The holding period restrictions for a national bank and an FSA are governed by different statutes and regulations, as explained in the next two sections.

The holding period begins on the date that

- ownership of the property is originally transferred to the bank and the redemption period, if any, has expired,
- a bank completes relocation from former banking premises to new banking premises, or ceases to use the former banking premises without relocating, or
- the bank decides not to use real estate acquired for future bank expansion.

Regardless of such restrictions, whenever a national bank or an FSA acquires OREO as the result of a merger with or an acquisition of another institution, the holding period of the newly acquired OREO commences on the date of merger or acquisition.

## National Banks

A national bank's holding period for OREO is governed by 12 USC 29 and 12 CFR 34.82. A national bank must dispose of OREO at the earliest time that prudent judgment dictates, but the holding period must be no longer than five years, unless the OCC grants the bank an extension. A national bank desiring an extension of the five-year holding period must file a request with and receive approval from the bank's OCC supervisory office. The OCC may grant multiple extensions, as long as those extensions, in the aggregate, do not exceed an additional five years. To receive an extension, the bank must be able to demonstrate to the OCC that it has made a good-faith effort to dispose of the property within the initial five-year period or that disposal of the property within the initial five-year period would be detrimental to the bank.

## Federal Savings Associations

An FSA's OREO holding period is addressed in 12 CFR 167.1 and 167.5. These regulations, which are part of the capital regulations governing FSAs, also address interests in real property acquired in satisfaction of debt previously contracted.

Under these regulations, FSAs deduct equity investments, which include equity investments in real property, from assets when calculating total capital. The term equity investment in real property does not include interests in real property used or intended to be used by the FSA for the conduct of its business, or property interests acquired in satisfaction of a debt previously contracted in good faith. In addition, the property must not be held for real estate investment purposes and should be disposed of within five years (or a longer period if approved by the OCC). In short, an FSA does not need to deduct from capital OREO that is not an equity investment in real property.

An FSA that wishes to retain OREO for more than five years and not deduct the value from capital must file a request with, and receive approval from, the FSA's OCC supervisory office. Approvals to retain OREO and not deduct the value from capital generally will not exceed an additional five years in the aggregate. There are no other regulatory requirements governing when an FSA must dispose of OREO. As with national banks, when requesting an extension, FSAs must be able to demonstrate to the OCC that it has made a good-faith effort to dispose of the property within the initial five-year period or that disposal of the property within the initial five-year period would be detrimental to the bank.

## Foreclosure Redemption Periods

As part of the foreclosure process, certain states have a mandatory period following a foreclosure sale during which the borrower can redeem its interest in the property by satisfying the debt. During this redemption period, the borrower generally has the right to occupy the property, thereby maintaining physical possession of the collateral. The length of the redemption period varies by state and often by property type, ranging from three months to one year. Although the bank has foreclosed on the property and, depending on the state, may have equitable or legal title, or both, the bank may not have possession before the expiration of the redemption period. The bank may sell its interest in the collateral during the redemption period, but this interest remains subject to the borrower's right of redemption.

Foreclosed real estate should be accounted for as OREO pursuant to generally accepted accounting principles (GAAP) and call report instructions without regard to any state redemption statutes. The five-year holding period does not, however, begin until the end of the redemption period, assuming the borrower does not redeem the property through payment in full. Banks should know the foreclosure and redemption statutes in all states in which they are active and manage OREO accordingly.

# Accounting

The Federal Financial Institutions Examination Council (FFIEC) call report instructions provide accounting guidance for OREO and other foreclosed assets. The instructions require that foreclosed assets be accounted for in accordance with GAAP. In this respect, ASC topic 310 and ASC topic 360 provide general guidance for the initial recording of foreclosed assets. ASC subtopic 970-340 provides guidance on the accounting for costs during a development and construction period, while ASC subtopic 835-20 provides guidance on capitalization of interest costs, if applicable. Sales of OREO are accounted for in accordance with ASC section 360-20-40. Accounting guidance for OREO can also be found, along with various scenarios with accounting entries, in the OCC's *Bank Accounting Advisory Series*.

## Accounting at Acquisition or Designation as OREO

Upon foreclosure or physical possession, whichever is earlier, OREO should be recorded at the fair value of the property, less the estimated cost to sell; this amount becomes the new cost basis of the property. The amount by which the recorded amount of the loan exceeds the new cost basis is a loss and must be charged to the allowance for loan and lease losses (ALLL). The recorded amount of the loan is the loan balance adjusted for any unamortized premium or discount and unamortized loan fees or costs, less any amount previously charged off, plus recorded accrued interest.

Other assets besides real property received in full satisfaction of a loan—such as motor vehicles, furniture and fixtures, equipment, financial instruments, and intangible assets—should be initially measured at the asset's fair value, less estimated cost to sell, if applicable, at the time of foreclosure or physical possession, whichever is earlier. As with OREO, the amount, if any, by which the recorded amount of the loan exceeds the fair value, less cost to sell, if applicable, must be charged to the ALLL. Refer to GAAP and the call report instructions for other accounting and reporting requirements for other foreclosed assets.

Assets received in partial satisfaction of a loan should be accounted for as previously described, and the recorded amount of the loan should be reduced by the fair value, less cost to sell if applicable, of the asset at the time of foreclosure.

A gain at the time of establishing OREO is rare. When a gain is recognized, the valuation supporting the fair value and estimated costs to sell should be closely reviewed.

If OREO is sold shortly after it is acquired, the amount of the loss originally charged to the ALLL may be adjusted for the value actually received in the sale (net of the cost to sell). "Shortly after" is generally defined as being before the filing of the next call report.

Former bank premises should be recorded at the lower of its net book value or fair value at the date of transfer to OREO. Any excess of net book value over fair value must be charged to expense of the current period.

An independent appraisal or evaluation, as appropriate, normally establishes the fair value of OREO and is discussed in the "Appraisals and Evaluations" section of this booklet. ASC 820-10 provides guidance on measuring the fair value. The valuation should be consistent with the price that a market participant will pay to purchase the property at the measurement date in its as-is condition. Circumstances such as changed economic conditions may indicate that the appraised value is not an accurate measurement of the property's current fair value and is no longer valid. See the "Appraisals and Evaluations" section for further discussion of the validity of appraisals and evaluations.

Costs incurred by a bank to perfect its lien before foreclosure may be eligible for inclusion in the recorded amount of the loan satisfied, subject to the bank recording the property at fair value, less estimated cost to sell. Examples of eligible costs are payments of delinquent property taxes to clear tax liens, payments to contractors and subcontractors to clear mechanic's liens, or paying off first lien positions on properties for which the bank holds the second lien. The bank should expense legal fees, filing fees, legal notice advertising costs, and other direct costs of acquiring title to the property when incurred.

When the bank acquires a parcel of property through foreclosure as a junior lienholder without paying off the senior lien,[2] the property should be booked at fair value, less costs to sell and the amount of any senior debt reported as a liability at the time of foreclosure. Any excess between the recorded amount of the loan plus the senior debt and the fair value of the property less costs to sell should be charged against the ALLL at the time of foreclosure.[3]

## Accounting for OREO During the Holding Period

Subsequent to acquisition and transfer, OREO must be carried at the lower of cost or fair value, less estimated costs to sell. Management should maintain documentation supporting each property's carrying value consistent with prudent banking practice and as required to ensure that quarterly regulatory reports are accurate and consistent with GAAP. Subsequent declines in fair value below the initial cost basis are recorded through the use of a valuation allowance. Subsequent recoveries of fair value before disposition of the property may be recognized up to the initial cost basis of the property established upon transfer to OREO, and may be recouped up to the amount of previously recognized valuation allowances established after acquisition.[4]

Changes in fair value must be determined on a property-by-property basis. An allowance allocated to one property may not be used to offset losses incurred on another property. Unallocated OREO valuation allowances are not acceptable. Subsequent increases in the fair value of a property may be used to reduce the valuation allowance, but not below zero. Banks may not include OREO valuation allowances as a component of tier 1 or tier 2 capital.

Generally, the revenues and expenses from OREO should be included in the income statement for the call report period in which they occur. The call report instructions require that gross rentals from OREO be included in other noninterest income. The expenses of operating or maintaining the property should be included in other noninterest expense. Normal OREO expenses include insurance, taxes, utilities, and routine maintenance and repairs. A bank may not recognize depreciation expense for assets held for sale, including OREO. ASC subtopic 970-340 permits certain expenses that are incurred during the

---

[2] If a junior lienholder forecloses and the senior mortgage remains, the junior lienholder is responsible for keeping the contractual payments on the senior mortgage note current.

[3] See the OCC's *Bank Accounting Advisory Series,* topic 5A.

[4] See the FFIEC call report instructions, RC-M-"Memoranda," item 3, "Other Real Estate Owned," for a discussion of valuation allowances for OREO.

completion of a project to be capitalized. See the "OREO expenditures" section of this booklet for more information.

## Accounting for Sales of OREO

The primary accounting guidance for sales of foreclosed real estate is ASC 360-20, "Property, Plant, and Equipment—Real Estate Sales" (formerly Financial Accounting Standards Board Statement 66, "Accounting for Sales of Real Estate").

ASC 360-20-40-7 describes the conditions that must be met for a transaction to qualify as a sale: (1) the parties are bound by the terms of a contract, (2) all consideration has been exchanged, (3) any permanent financing for which the seller is responsible has been arranged, and (4) all conditions precedent to closing have been performed. A transaction need only qualify as a sale under GAAP as described in ASC 360-20-40-7 to transfer the asset out of OREO, even when the seller finances 100 percent of the purchase price.

ASC 360-20, which applies to all transactions in which the seller provides financing to the buyer of the real estate, establishes five methods to account for dispositions of real estate. If a profit (gain) is involved in the sale of the real estate, each method sets forth the manner in which the profit is to be recognized. Regardless of which method is used, any losses on the disposition of real estate must be recognized immediately.

**Full accrual method:** Under the full accrual method, the disposition is recorded as a sale. Any profit resulting from the sale is recognized in full and the asset resulting from the seller's financing of the transaction is reported as a loan. This method may be used when the following conditions have been met:

- A sale has been consummated.
- The buyer's initial investment (down payment) and continuing investment (periodic payments) are adequate to demonstrate a commitment to pay for the property.
- The receivable is not subject to future subordination.
- The usual risks and rewards of ownership have been transferred.

Guidelines for the minimum down payment that must be made for a transaction to qualify for the full accrual method are described in ASC 360-20-55-2, appendix A. These vary from 5 percent to 25 percent of the property's sales value.[5] These guideline percentages vary by type of property and are primarily based on the inherent risk assumed for the type and characteristics of the property. To meet the continuing investment criteria, the contractual loan payments must be sufficient to repay the loan over the customary loan term for the type of property involved. Such periods may range up to 30 years for loans on single-family residential properties.

---

[5] Sales value is the sales price adjusted by certain additions and deductions. See ASC 360-20-40-8 for instructions on determination of sales value.

**Installment method:** Dispositions of foreclosed real estate that do not qualify for the full accrual method may qualify for the installment method. This method recognizes a sale and the corresponding loan. Any profits on the sale are recognized only as the bank receives payments from the purchaser/borrower. Interest income is recognized on an accrual basis, when appropriate.

The installment method is used when the buyer's down payment is not adequate to allow use of the full accrual method but recovery of the cost of the property is reasonably assured if the buyer defaults. Assurance of recovery requires careful judgment on a case-by-case basis. Factors that should be considered include the size of the down payment, loan-to-value ratios, projected cash flows from the property, recourse provisions, and guarantees.

Because default on the loan usually results in the seller's reacquisition of the real estate, reasonable assurance of cost recovery may often be achieved with a relatively small down payment. This is especially true in situations involving loans with recourse to borrowers who have verifiable net worth, liquid assets, and income levels. Reasonable assurance of cost recovery may also be achieved when the purchaser/borrower pledges additional collateral.

**Cost recovery method:** Dispositions of foreclosed real estate that do not qualify for the full accrual or installment methods are sometimes accounted for using the cost recovery method. This method recognizes a sale and the corresponding loan, but all income recognition is deferred. Principal payments are applied as reductions of the loan balance, and interest increases the unrecognized gross profit. No profit or interest income is recognized until either the aggregate payments by the borrower exceed the recorded amount of the loan or a change to another accounting method (e.g., the installment method) is appropriate. Consequently, the loan is maintained in nonaccrual status while this method is being used.

**Reduced-profit method:** This method is used in certain situations in which the bank receives an adequate down payment but the loan amortization schedule does not meet the requirements for use of the full accrual method. The method recognizes a sale and the corresponding loan; like the installment method, however, any profit is apportioned over the life of the loan as payments are received. The method of apportionment differs from the installment method in that profit recognition is based on the present value of the lowest level of periodic payments required under the loan agreement. Because sales with adequate down payments are generally not structured with inadequate loan amortization requirements, this method is seldom used.

**Deposit method:** The deposit method is used in situations where a sale of the foreclosed real estate has not been consummated. This method may also be used for dispositions that could be accounted for under the cost recovery method. A sale is not recorded and the asset continues to be reported as foreclosed real estate. Further, no profit or interest income is recognized. Payments received from the borrower are reported as liabilities until sufficient payments or other events have occurred that allow the use of one of the other methods.

The preceding discussion represents a brief summary of the methods included in ASC 360-20 for accounting for sales of real estate. Refer to ASC 360-20 for a more complete description of the accounting principles that apply to sales of real estate, including the determination of the down payment percentage. The OCC's *Bank Accounting Advisory Series* provides additional guidance on accounting for the disposition of OREO.

## Appraisals and Evaluations

12 CFR 34.85 and 12 CFR 160.172 establish the appraisal requirements for OREO held by national banks and FSAs, respectively. Appraisal requirements are also defined by 12 CFR 34, subpart C-Appraisals (national banks), 12 CFR 164, "Appraisals" (FSAs), and OCC Bulletin 2010-42, "Sound Practices for Appraisals and Evaluations: Interagency Appraisal and Evaluation Guidelines" (national banks and FSAs).

12 CFR 34.85 and 12 CFR 160.172 require national banks and FSAs, respectively, to obtain an appraisal or evaluation, as appropriate, to substantiate the market value of each parcel upon transfer to OREO.[6] If a bank has a valid and compliant appraisal or evaluation that was previously obtained in connection with the real estate loan, however, the bank does not need to obtain a new appraisal or evaluation to comply with these regulations. Section XIV, "Validity of Appraisals and Evaluations," of the *Interagency Appraisal and Evaluation Guidelines*,[7] states that banks should establish criteria for assessing whether an existing appraisal or evaluation remains valid and discusses factors that should be considered in such an assessment. Factors to be considered should include, but are not limited to

- passage of time.
- volatility of the local market.
- changes in terms and availability of financing.
- natural disasters.
- limited or over supply of competing properties.
- improvements to the subject property or competing properties.
- lack of maintenance of the subject or competing properties.
- changes in underlying economic and market assumptions, such as capitalization rates and lease terms.
- changes in zoning, building materials, or technology.
- environmental contamination.

The application of an arbitrary period of time, such as 12 months, should not be used as stand-alone criteria for determining the validity of an appraisal or an evaluation. The passage of time is just one component of that assessment and other factors that affect value must be considered in making such a determination.

---

[6] A bank may substantiate a property's market value by obtaining an appropriate evaluation when the recorded investment in the loan satisfied is equal to or less than $250,000. Requirements for an appropriate evaluation are described in 12 CFR 34.85, 12 CFR 160.172, and OCC Bulletin 2010-42, "Sound Practices for Appraisals and Evaluations: Interagency Appraisal and Evaluation Guidelines."

[7] OCC Bulletin 2010-42, "Sound Practices for Appraisals and Evaluations: Interagency Appraisal and Evaluation Guidelines."

The bank should maintain documentation that provides the facts and analysis used to support the bank's conclusion that an existing appraisal or evaluation remains valid and appropriate to establish the property's current market value.

In circumstances when the bank transfers the property to OREO but does not yet have access to the interior of the property, an exterior-only appraisal may be performed utilizing an extraordinary assumption regarding the interior condition of the property to fulfill the requirements under 12 CFR 34.85 and 12 CFR 160.172. Once access is obtained, the bank should inspect the property to determine if the assumption, and appraisal, remain valid. If conditions warrant, an updated appraisal should be performed.

National banks are not required to obtain a new appraisal or evaluation when selling OREO if the sale is consummated based on a valid appraisal or evaluation as described in 12 CFR 34.85(c). FSAs are not expressly required under 12 CFR 160.172 to obtain an appraisal or evaluation when selling OREO; however, the sale of OREO constitutes a real estate-related financial transaction under 12 CFR 164, and, as such, the sale must be supported by a new or valid existing appraisal or evaluation, as appropriate.

A bank must have an appropriate and effective appraisal and evaluation policy for OREO. The policy should require the monitoring of OREO values in a manner consistent with prudent banking practice; this should include appropriate periodic reviews of the property throughout a property's holding period. These reviews should substantiate the carrying value of the property. Appraisals and evaluations should be reviewed and the reviews should be documented in writing and approved by authorities defined in the bank's appraisal policy. Examiners should review the adequacy of a bank's OREO appraisal policy and determine if bank staff responsible for managing OREO complies with the bank's policy and applicable laws and regulations. The OCC may require a bank to obtain a new appraisal or evaluation when the agency believes it is necessary to address safety and soundness concerns.

## Management and Disposition

### OREO Expenditures

Under certain circumstances, national banks and FSAs may make additional expenditures on OREO. The authority for national banks to engage in this activity is in 12 USC 29 and 12 CFR 34, while an FSA's inherent or implied salvage powers allow the FSA to engage in this activity.

### National Banks

12 USC 29 grants the power for a national bank to expend funds to develop and improve OREO so the bank may recover its total investment, subject to conditions and limitations prescribed by the OCC. 12 CFR 34.86 establishes requirements relating to additional expenditures on OREO and certain notification procedures. For OREO that is a development or improvement project, 12 CFR 34.86(a) states that a national bank can make advances to complete the project if the advances are

- reasonably calculated to reduce the shortfall between the property's market value and the bank's recorded investment amount.
- not made for speculative purposes.
- consistent with safe and sound practices.

When the sum of a development or improvement plan's estimated cost plus the bank's current recorded investment amount (including any unpaid prior liens) exceeds10 percent of the bank's capital and surplus, the regulation requires a national bank to notify the OCC at least 30 days before implementing the development or improvement plan.

The required notification must demonstrate that the additional expenditure is consistent with the conditions and limitations set forth at 12 CFR 34.86(a). Unless otherwise informed by the OCC, the national bank may implement the plan on the 31st day (or sooner if notified by the OCC) after the OCC receives the bank's notification, subject to any conditions imposed by the OCC. The notification procedures state that a national bank does not need to notify the OCC of refit costs for new tenants in an existing building or of expenditures necessary for ordinary repairs and maintenance that protect the value of the property.

## Federal Savings Associations

An FSA's salvage powers are not governed by regulation but are deemed to be inherent or implied and, in certain circumstances, permit the FSA to hold, operate, and invest additional funds in property acquired as a result of, or in lieu of, foreclosure before resale of the property. These powers permit the FSA to take whatever steps necessary to salvage an investment, provided the steps taken are integral parts of a reasonable and bona fide salvage plan and do not contravene a specific legal prohibition. The FSA may exceed its lending limit[8] in exercising its salvage powers, provided the FSA is able to demonstrate that it is making the excess investment pursuant to a reasonable and bona fide salvage plan. Excess investments that are not made pursuant to such a plan are not permitted and could prompt enforcement action.

An FSA that intends to make a salvage powers investment that, when aggregated with the FSA's recorded investment in the property, would exceed its lending limit must file a request with, and receive no objection from, the OCC. While subsequent expenditures made on properties that have been acquired in satisfaction of debt are not considered for the purpose of loan-to-one-borrower limitations, the OCC may consider these expenditures in identifying significant salvage activities that may require special scrutiny.

When reviewing a proposed salvage plan request, the OCC takes into consideration the risks posed by the proposed salvage plan, the FSA's past history of salvage operations, and the FSA's financial condition and ability to undertake the risks attendant to salvage operations. In addition, the OCC considers whether the proposed salvage plan meets the following criteria:

---

[8] 12 CFR 32, "Lending Limits," establishes limits for both national banks and FSAs.

- Is it necessary to enable the FSA to salvage its existing investment?
- Is it necessary to protect the value of the foreclosed property (e.g., the additional investments will result in a more marketable property)?
- Is it in the best interest of the FSA?
- Will it reduce the risks associated with the foreclosed property?
- Is it for nonspeculative purposes?

## Other OREO Expenditure Considerations Applicable to National Banks and FSAs

For both national banks and FSAs, costs incurred to complete construction may be capitalized; however, the recorded balance of the OREO should not exceed the "as-completed" fair value, less estimated costs to sell. The bank should monitor the remaining cost to complete construction to ensure the actual cost will not exceed original estimates. The recorded OREO balance should never exceed fair value, less estimated costs to sell.

In reviewing OREO expenditures by national banks or FSAs, the OCC considers several factors. The completion of unfinished construction may be justified if significant funds have already been expended and completion is likely to result in enhanced recovery of funds. Completion of projects that are far from complete would typically not be approved and would require a careful analysis of the facts supporting the expenditures.

Ground-up construction of buildings including out-parcels and separate structures in a development usually would not be approved absent extenuating circumstances. Circumstances may include preleased commercial buildings or presold residences and the construction of common buildings, such as clubhouses, where there is compelling evidence that a significant number of real estate closings are dependent on their completion.

Speculative lot development would not normally be approved. Completion of partially developed lots may be approved, however, especially if there are builder commitments in place to purchase the lots. If prospects for selling lots in the foreseeable future are poor, additional expenditures usually should not be incurred. Expenditures required by government entities (i.e. when the owner has no choice) for erosion control and completion of other mandated site improvements are generally allowable.

## Managing Foreclosed Properties

When establishing and implementing policies and procedures necessary to address the new and expanded risks presented by the management of foreclosed properties, bank management and the board of directors should consider, at a minimum, the following.

## Obligations and Actions

- In acquiring title to foreclosed properties, a bank assumes the primary responsibilities of an owner, including providing maintenance and security, paying taxes and insurance, and serving as landlord for rental properties.
  - The bank should communicate with localities, including homeowners' associations, about specific requirements with respect to foreclosed residential properties. For example, localities may have requirements for upkeep—such as lawn mowing, property maintenance, and security—and the requirements may become applicable at different stages of the foreclosure process.
  - If it fails to take these actions, the bank should be aware of potential nuisance actions or the exercise of local receivership powers to seize properties.
- For Federal Housing Administration (FHA)-insured mortgages, the bank must ensure compliance with property and preservation guidance issued by the U.S. Department of Housing and Urban Development (HUD) to preserve the insurance claim and obtain reimbursements for allowable expenses.
- Following foreclosure, the bank must record its ownership interest in local land records.
- Banks must comply with OREO appraisal and accounting requirements.
- Banks should maintain appropriate insurance on the property.
- Some localities may require registration of foreclosed properties, properties in foreclosure, or vacant properties. Banks should be aware of and comply with such requirements.
- The Protecting Tenants at Foreclosure Act of 2009 provides tenants with protections from eviction resulting from foreclosure on the properties they are renting. The "Protecting Tenants at Foreclosure Act" booklet of the *Comptroller's Handbook* provides additional information and examination guidance.
  - When a bank takes title to a house after foreclosure, it must honor any existing rental agreement with a bona fide tenant and must provide 90 days' notice to the tenant before eviction, whether or not the tenant has a rental agreement.
  - State laws may impose additional requirements that are not preempted by the Protecting Tenants at Foreclosure Act.
  - Additional potential requirements with respect to rental properties include
    - reviewing the lease to determine if the property can be shown to prospective purchasers.
    - returning any security deposit upon termination of the rental agreement.
- The Servicemembers Civil Relief Act provides servicemembers relief from certain obligations when military service affects the servicemember's ability to meet or attend to civil matters. The "Servicemembers Civil Relief Act" booklet of the *Comptroller's Handbook* provides additional information and examination guidance.
  - Real property acquired by a servicemember before the servicemember's military service began cannot be sold, foreclosed, or seized during the period of military service and for a period subsequent to the military service. Prior to December 31, 2014, the period extends an additional year. Subsequent to December 31, 2014, the extension period reverts to 90 days. These restrictions can be superseded with the approval of a court or a written agreement in which the servicemember agrees to waive certain rights.

- A landlord may not evict a servicemember or his or her dependents from certain residences[9] occupied primarily as a residence during a period of military service except by court order.

## Additional Issues

- Banks should have sufficient staff to manage foreclosed property portfolios and policies, procedures, and risk management systems in place to properly oversee and manage third-party relationships. The use of third parties does not diminish the responsibility of the board of directors and management to ensure that foreclosed properties are administered in a safe and sound manner and in compliance with applicable law. Third-party relationships should be subject to the same risk management process that would be expected if a bank were conducting the activities directly. Such a risk management process should include
  - written contracts outlining the duties, obligations, and responsibilities of the parties involved.
  - appropriate due diligence before entering a third-party contract.
  - continuous oversight of the third parties and third-party activities.
- Before undertaking the rehabilitation or improvement of foreclosed properties, a bank should consider its legal authority to make expenditures on OREO and any HUD requirements for mortgages insured by the FHA. For FHA-insured loans, such expenditures are permissible if reasonably calculated to reduce any shortfall between the parcel's market value and the bank's recorded investment amount. If such expenditures are permissible and the bank makes them, the bank should ensure compliance with local building codes and licensing requirements.
- When disposing of foreclosed residential properties, a bank should consider
  - disposition costs and delays, including advertising, broker, or maintenance fees and repair costs for defects found at inspection.
  - the provision of financing for OREO properties. While generally not subject to lending limits, financing the sale of a significant number of properties to the same borrower could result in unsafe or unsound concentrations.
  - negative reaction and potential reputation risk from disposition practices that favor, as purchasers of foreclosed properties, investors (paying cash) over owner-occupants (paying with financing).
  - opportunities to participate in and coordinate with state and local land bank programs, neighborhood stabilization programs, redevelopment programs, and other anti-blight programs, or opportunities to enhance owner occupancy.
- When disposing of foreclosed residential properties from FHA-insured mortgages, either through sales or conveyance to HUD, the bank must comply with HUD requirements to receive insurance payments or other allowable reimbursements.
- Holding-period issues may arise if the bank is not able to dispose of foreclosed properties.

---

[9] For leased residences, the law, as originally passed by Congress, applied to dwellings with monthly rents not exceeding a certain amount. This amount is adjusted yearly and is published in the *Federal Register* by the U.S. Department of Defense. The amount as of January 1, 2013, was $3,139.35 (78 Fed. Reg. 9678).

In addition to the guidance provided above, appendix B contains guidance for managing foreclosed properties when a bank is acting as the servicer of foreclosed property and when the bank is the trustee of a securitization trust that holds title to foreclosed property.

## Releasing a Lien Rather Than Foreclosing

At times, lenders may release a lien securing a defaulted residential real estate loan rather than foreclose on the property. This decision is often based on financial considerations, such as when the bank or servicer/investor determines that the costs to foreclose, rehabilitate, and sell a property exceed its current market value. When this decision is made after a bank or servicer has initiated foreclosure, the borrower may have already abandoned the property or discontinued the care and maintenance of the property, increasing the chance of a blighted property in the community. Because the decision to release a lien is typically a financial decision, banks and servicers should ensure that their valuation of the property provides the best information practicable, while complying with investor requirements, before initiating foreclosure and subsequently deciding to release the lien. While the financial risk must be considered, banks and servicers should also consider the potential for reputation and litigation risk arising from their position as a prior mortgagee or servicer of a now-abandoned property.

If the decision is made to forego foreclosure and release the lien, the bank or servicer should notify, or attempt to notify, the borrower of the decision. Borrowers should be notified that (1) the mortgage holder is not pursuing foreclosure and has released the mortgage lien, (2) the borrower may continue to occupy the property, and (3) the borrower is obligated to maintain the property consistent with all local codes and ordinances and to pay property taxes and the debt owed. The bank or servicer should also make appropriate notifications to the local jurisdiction when it makes the decision to release a lien in lieu of foreclosure.

## Exchanging OREO for Other Assets

A weak economic environment can lead to significant deterioration in asset quality resulting in an increase in lower-quality assets, including OREO. When this occurs, third parties may market OREO exchange programs to a bank as a means of reducing problem assets. These programs purport to reduce nonperforming assets by exchanging OREO for an interest in another asset that may be represented to be of higher quality. This "higher quality asset" is often an equity interest in the entity acquiring the OREO or a trade for a large number of loans, such as home equity lines of credit. These programs can raise significant safety and soundness, legal, and accounting concerns, and the OCC strongly encourages banks to consult with their OCC supervisory office before entering into any such agreements. Additional information on this topic is included in appendix A of this booklet.

## Rental of Residential OREO

The OCC supports a bank's efforts to obtain the highest recovery possible on residential OREO while also considering the impact of OREO disposition on the communities the bank serves. In general, banks must dispose of OREO as prudent judgment dictates and within the holding period permitted by law or regulation. If the bank can recover the recorded loan amount as well as recorded accrued interest, additional advances, and other costs, it should promptly dispose of the property.

In certain markets, however, the bank's analysis may support renting homes for a reasonable period of time, generally one year or less, as part of a prudent disposition strategy. If the bank employs such a strategy, it must demonstrate and document diligent, reasonable, and ongoing sales efforts.

A rental program should be executed under an appropriate risk management framework that is commensurate with the size and scope of the program and is designed to control the heightened reputation, credit, operational, and compliance risks that can arise when a bank becomes a landlord. This framework includes complying with federal, state, and local laws that govern rental agreements and tenant rights. Specific controls should include

- comprehensive written policy objectives and operating procedures governing OREO recognition, carrying values, management and maintenance, and disposition.
- reporting systems that track OREO flows, volumes, and disposition status (including any rental programs).
- accounting and reporting for rental OREO in accordance with existing regulatory reporting requirements.
- active oversight of any third parties that assist with the management and disposition of OREO properties, as described in OCC Bulletin 2001-47, "Third-Party Relationships: Risk Management Principles."
- control systems (audit, quality assurance, legal reviews, etc.) with sufficient scope, review schedules, and expertise to ensure compliance with all pertinent federal, state, and local laws.[10]

## Disposition of OREO

12 CFR 34.83, "Disposition of real estate" describes how a national bank may comply with its legal obligation to dispose of real estate under 12 USC 29. Disposition by FSAs is governed similarly by policy. A bank may dispose of OREO by

- entering into a sale in accordance with GAAP.
- entering into a transaction that involves a loan guaranteed or insured by the U.S. government or by an agency of the U.S. government, or a loan eligible for purchase by a federally sponsored instrumentality that purchases loans.
- selling the property pursuant to a land contract or a contract for deed.

---

[10] These laws include landlord-tenant laws; landlord licensing or registration requirements; minimum leasing requirements; eviction protections under the Protecting Tenants at Foreclosure Act; protections under the Servicemembers Civil Relief Act; reasonable accommodation and accessibility requirements for handicapped or disabled tenants under the Fair Housing Act and the Americans With Disabilities Act; antidiscrimination laws, including the Fair Housing Act; and other standards associated with providing clean, sanitary, and safe properties.

- with respect to real estate acquired in exchange for debts previously contracted, retaining the property for its own use as bank premises or by transferring it to a subsidiary or affiliate for use in the business of the subsidiary or affiliate.

A bank must make diligent and ongoing efforts to dispose of each parcel of OREO and maintain documentation adequate to reflect those efforts.

With respect to a capitalized or operating lease, a bank may dispose of its interest by either assigning the lease or subleasing the premises to a third party. If a bank enters into a sublease that expires before the master (original) lease—i.e., it is not coterminous—the period during which the master lease must be divested is suspended for the duration of the sublease and begins running again upon expiration or termination of the sublease. A bank holding a lease as OREO may enter into an extension of the OREO holding period if the extension meets the following criteria:

- The extension is necessary in order to sublease the master lease.
- The bank, before entering into the extension, has a firm commitment from a prospective subtenant to sublease the property.
- The term of the extension is reasonable and does not materially exceed the term of the sublease.[11]

With respect to a transaction that does not qualify as a disposition, a disposition is considered to be achieved when the bank receives or accumulates from the purchaser an amount in a down payment, principal and interest payments, and private mortgage insurance totaling at least 10 percent of the sales price, as measured by GAAP.

While the OCC does not prescribe specific methods to be used, such as listing a property with a broker, examiners will evaluate the effectiveness of a bank's marketing program in assessing the diligence of the bank's efforts to dispose of OREO.

## Concentrations

Concentration risk in OREO should be considered together with similar real estate concentrations that may be present in the loan portfolio. The OCC's "Concentrations of Credit" booklet of the *Comptroller's Handbook* defines a concentration as exceeding 25 percent of tier 1 risk-based capital plus the ALLL and contains additional information and guidance in assessing concentrations. OCC Bulletin 2006-46, "Concentrations in Commercial Real Estate Lending, Sound Risk Management Practices: Interagency Guidance on CRE Concentration Risk Management," provides guidance on the management of concentrations in commercial real estate.

---

[11] 12 CFR 34.83 states that, should the OCC determine that a bank has entered into a lease, extension of a lease, or a sublease for the purpose of real estate speculation in violation of 12 USC 29 and this part, the OCC will take appropriate measures to address the violation, which may include requiring the bank to take immediate steps to divest the lease or sublease.

A bank's holding of OREO may represent concentrations in specific types of real estate or in specific geographic locations. The bank's management information system should permit analysis of the OREO portfolio for concentrations. Management should identify and separately analyze the types of properties that are included in the account, the aging of properties (e.g., how many were acquired in the last year, the last three years, or the last five years), and management's efforts to sell the properties. Management should also identify geographic concentrations of OREO even though the types of real estate may be different, because economic conditions in a particular geographic location may pose similar risks to different types of real estate.

## Environmental Risk Management

An effective environmental risk management policy that assesses a property's environmental risk before extending a loan is an important element of sound risk management. A bank should, however, also have appropriate environmental risk management policies and procedures in place for OREO as a part of its overall environmental risk management program. Property use may have changed, an adequate assessment may not have been performed at origination, contamination may not have been evident, a property may have become contaminated subsequent to loan closing, or the bank may be exposed to expanded liability as an owner of a contaminated property.

A bank's OREO policy should establish a program for assessing the potential adverse effect of environmental contamination and ensure appropriate controls to limit the bank's exposure to environmental liability from OREO. In addition to federal laws and regulations, states usually have their own environmental laws and regulations, and loan officers and risk managers should be familiar with the laws and regulations in their market areas. The "Commercial Real Estate Lending" booklet of the *Comptroller's Handbook* provides a more detailed discussion of the risks presented by contaminated properties and supervisory expectations for mitigating these risks.

Although seldom an issue with residential properties, with the possible exception of lead-based paint, the risk posed by contamination of commercial properties can be significant. Environmental contamination may negatively affect the value of real property collateral as well as create potential liability for the bank under various federal or state environmental laws. Appraisals or evaluations must recognize and evaluate known property contamination and include this assessment in estimates of market value.

## Regulatory Risk Rating

The risk rating of OREO by banks should be consistent with the interagency "Uniform Agreement on the Classification of Assets and Appraisal of Securities Held by Banks and Thrifts" conveyed by OCC Bulletin 2004-25, "Classification of Securities: Uniform Agreement on the Classification of Securities," and, for FSAs, 12 CFR 160.160, "Asset Classification." While it is not OCC policy to automatically classify OREO, such assets are normally of lower quality, even when carried at or below their fair value, less costs to sell. A bank's purchase of property through foreclosure usually indicates a lack of demand for the property, and a bank often suffers a loss when disposing of OREO despite the apparent adequacy of appraised values. OREO is often a nonearning asset, and the bank incurs costs to hold the property such as property taxes, insurance, utilities, repairs, and maintenance. The bank may also incur substantial liability generated by environmental issues.

During supervisory examinations of a bank, OREO should be evaluated to determine the appropriate regulatory risk ratings. An examiner should review all relevant factors to determine the amount of risk presented by each parcel of OREO and the probability that the bank will realize the OREO's carrying value. Factors an examiner should consider as part of the evaluation include

- the property's carrying value relative to its fair value, the bank's asking price, and offers received. For example, a carrying value in excess of fair value would indicate a loss, an asking price significantly above the carrying value may discourage offers or indicate a bank's unwillingness to sell at the carrying value, and offers that are significantly below the asking price may indicate that the carrying value or asking price is too high. Any of these could reduce the probability of realizing the carrying value.
- the quality and timeliness of the property's appraisal or evaluation.
- the length of time the property has been on the market and local market conditions for the type of property involved, such as the history and recent sales trends for comparable properties.
- management's ability and track record in disposing of foreclosed assets.
- the income generated by the property and other economic factors affecting the probability of loss exposure; generally, assets need to generate a reasonable net return commensurate with similar risk assets to warrant a pass classification.
- other pertinent factors, including title, statutory redemption privileges, zoning, and other liens.

OREO is normally treated as a substandard asset because of the collateral-dependent nature of the asset, the disposition risks, and fluctuations in market value. Banks should evaluate rental properties on a case-by-case basis, giving consideration to income generated and all expenses of ownership when making the classification determination. The appraisal or evaluation of the property may provide useful guidance in evaluating the adequacy of the property expenses and rate of return expectations used in support of the rating. Generally, assets need to generate a reasonable net return commensurate with similar-risk assets to warrant a pass classification.

# Examination Procedures

This booklet contains expanded procedures for examining specialized activities or specific products or services that warrant attention beyond the core assessment contained in the "Community Bank Supervision," "Large Bank Supervision," and "Federal Branches and Agencies Supervision" booklets of the *Comptroller's Handbook*. Examiners determine which expanded procedures to use, if any, during examination planning or after drawing preliminary conclusions during the core assessment.

## Scope

These procedures are designed to help examiners tailor the examination to each bank and determine the scope of the OREO examination. This determination should consider (1) work performed by internal and external auditors and by other examiners in related areas and (2) other independent risk control functions. Examiners need to perform only those objectives and steps that are relevant to the scope of the examination as determined by the following objectives. Seldom is every objective or step of the expanded procedures necessary.

The examiner conducting the OREO examination should work closely with the loan portfolio management (LPM) examiner to identify mutual areas of concern and to maximize examination efficiencies. Much of the information required to perform these procedures is available from the LPM examiner. OREO issues that pose a challenge to management or present unusual or significant risk to the bank should be included in comments on risk management and asset quality.

**Objective:** To determine the scope of the OREO examination and identify examination objectives and activities necessary to meet the needs of the supervisory strategy for the bank.

1. Review the following sources of information and note any previously identified problems related to OREO that require follow-up:

   - Supervisory strategy
   - Examiner-in-charge's (EIC) scope memorandum
   - OCC information systems (Examiner View or WISDM)
   - Previous reports of examination (ROE) and work papers
   - Internal and external audit reports and work papers
   - Bank management's responses to previous ROE and audit reports
   - Customer complaints and litigation

2. Obtain and review the Uniform Bank Performance Report (UBPR), Bank Expert Report (BERT), and other OCC reports. Review OREO levels and growth rates, trends in the classification of real estate loans, and other factors that can assist in assessing the risk presented by OREO.

3.  Obtain and review policies, procedures, and reports that bank management uses to supervise OREO, including internal risk assessments and relevant board or committee minutes.

4.  In discussions with bank management, determine whether there have been any significant changes (in policies, processes, personnel, control systems, products, volumes, markets, geographies, etc.) since the prior OREO examination.

5.  Based on an analysis of information obtained in the previous steps, as well as input from the EIC and LPM, if applicable, determine the scope and objectives of the OREO examination.

6.  Select from the following examination procedures the steps necessary to meet examination objectives and the core assessment.

# Quantity of Risk

## Conclusion: The quantity of each associated risk is (low, moderate, or high).

**Objective:** To determine the quantity of price risk associated with OREO activities.

1. Consider the following in forming your conclusion:

   - The amount of OREO and trends in the bank's volume of acquisition and disposition.
   - The amount and trend of OREO as a percentage of capital.
   - Real estate market conditions and trends.
   - The effectiveness of the bank's disposition efforts.

2. Ensure that management has accurately identified all OREO assets by discussing the following with the loan portfolio manager and the examiners assigned to review the allowance for loan and lease losses and bank premises and equipment:

   - Does the bank hold any real estate acquired in full or partial satisfaction of debt?
   - Are there vacated bank premises or property originally purchased for future expansion that is no longer intended for such usage?
   - Does the bank report as OREO properties of which it has physical possession, even if it does not have title?
   - Does the bank report as OREO properties for which it has received title, regardless of whether the properties are in statutory redemption periods?
   - Does the bank report as OREO equity interests that it may have in special purpose entities (SPE) that hold OREO?
   - Are there OREO sales that did not qualify for sales treatment according to GAAP?

3. Guided by examiner judgment, prepare a sample of OREO for analysis. From bank credit files, liability records, and internal reports, transcribe the following information to line sheets for each property:

   - A description of the property.
   - The date that title—or possession if this occurred prior to title—was obtained and when the asset was recorded as OREO.
   - The method of acquisition.
   - The current book value and balance at establishment of OREO.
   - The amount and date of the most recent appraisal or evaluation.
   - The bank's asking price and the dates and amounts of any offers.
   - The amount of insurance (including liability coverage), whether it is adequate and whether the bank is named as the insured (or as loss payee if title has not yet been acquired).
   - Dates and findings of inspection reports.

- Dates and findings of environmental reports.
- Whether the property is subject to a statutory redemption period.
- Whether the property is occupied.
- Whether the property is subject to a lease.
- Income and expense records, if applicable.
- A list of expenditures made to improve the property.
  - For national banks, where the sum of the bank's recorded investment amount plus the expenditures (including any unpaid prior liens) exceeds 10 percent of the bank's capital and surplus, indicate whether the bank obtained prior OCC approval. Note whether each expenditure is
    - reasonably calculated to reduce the shortfall between the property's market value and book value.
    - not made for speculative purposes.
    - consistent with safe and sound practices.
  - For expenditures by FSAs, if the sum of the book value and expenditure would be over its lending limit, note whether the FSA received a non-objection letter from the OCC. For each expenditure, note whether the expenditure
    - is necessary to enable the FSA to salvage its existing investment.
    - is necessary to protect the value of the foreclosed property (e.g., the additional investments will result in a more marketable property).
    - is in the best interest of the FSA.
    - will reduce the risks associated with the foreclosed property.
    - is not made for speculative purposes.

4. Determine whether the bank reviews properties for possible environmental contamination and deterioration in physical condition that might affect the value of the property. Investigate actions management has taken, or is in the process of taking, to address these conditions when they have discovered them.

5. Through discussions with management, assign appropriate risk ratings. Forward a list of OREO classifications, including write-ups, where necessary, to the EIC or LPM examiner.

**Objective:** To determine the quantity of liquidity risk associated with OREO activities.

1. Determine this risk by considering the following:

- A comparison of the amount and volume trends of OREO with the bank's liquidity levels and anticipated liquidity needs.
- The composition of the OREO portfolio and the volume of OREO disposition.
- A comparison of the volume of cash sales and financed sales.
- Market conditions and trends.

**Objective:** To determine the quantity of operational risk associated with OREO activities.

1. Determine the effect of the following on operational risk as it relates to the acquisition, holding, and disposition of OREO:

   - The amount, volume, type and trend of OREO; consider both acquisition and disposition.
   - The amount and trend of operational losses resulting from inadequate or failed internal processes or systems, the misconduct or errors of people, and adverse external events.
   - The volume and severity of operational, administrative, personnel, and accounting control errors.
   - The effectiveness of the bank's appraisal and evaluation program.
   - The quality and independence of the audit and asset review functions.
   - The adequacy of staffing, both in number and level of expertise.
   - The adequacy of OREO information systems and reports.
   - The volume and types of activities that are performed by third parties.
   - The adequacy of systems to properly select, oversee and manage third-party relationships.
   - The bank's strategies with respect to acquiring, holding and marketing OREO.
   - External factors including market conditions and any legislative, regulatory, or accounting changes.

**Objective:** To determine the quantity of compliance risk associated with OREO activities.

1. Review each parcel in the sample to determine whether the bank accounts for and reports OREO in accordance with GAAP and call report instructions.

2. Review each parcel in the sample to determine compliance with applicable laws and regulations as discussed in the "Introduction" section and cited in the "References" section of this booklet.

3. For each parcel of OREO that has been held more than five years or beyond any formally approved extension of the five-year holding period, determine if the bank obtained appropriate approval from its OCC supervisory office.

4. Review each parcel of OREO in the sample to determine if appropriate measures have been taken to identify and manage risks presented by environmental contamination.

5. Assess the bank's knowledge of and compliance with state or local laws that govern its ownership of property and its obligations regarding contaminated properties.

6. Assess the bank's knowledge of and compliance with the Fair Housing Act, Protecting Tenants at Foreclosure Act, and the Servicemembers Civil Relief Act.

7. Investigate any OREO insider transactions. If any exist, consult with the examiners performing the review of insider activities or related organizations.

**Objective:** To determine the level of reputation risk associated with OREO activities.

1. Reach a conclusion by considering the following:

   - The number, value, and types of OREO.
   - The volume of foreclosures and the bank's foreclosure practices.
   - The volume and nature of litigation related to OREO activities.
   - The impact of the bank's property management practices on neighborhoods and communities where the bank holds OREO.
   - The effect of disposition practices that favor investors (paying cash) over owner-occupants (purchasing with financing).
   - Participation in and coordination, or lack thereof, with state and local land bank programs, neighborhood stabilization programs, redevelopment programs, and other anti-blight programs or opportunities to enhance owner occupancy.

# Quality of Risk Management

## Conclusion: The quality of risk management is (strong, satisfactory, or weak).

The conclusion on risk management considers all risks associated with OREO activities.

## Policies

Policies are statements of actions adopted by a bank to pursue certain objectives. Policies often set standards (on risk tolerances, for example) and should be consistent with the bank's underlying mission, values, and principles. A policy review should always be triggered when the bank's objectives or standards change.

**Objective:** To determine whether the board has adopted effective policies that are consistent with safe and sound banking practices and appropriate to the size, nature, and scope of the bank's OREO portfolio.

1. Evaluate OREO policies to determine whether they provide appropriate guidance for managing the bank's OREO and are consistent with the bank's mission, values, and principles.

   - Determine whether the bank's policies provide guidance consistent with
     - a bank's statutory authority to hold OREO.
     - statutes governing permitted holding periods.
     - statutes and regulations governing property management and disposition.
     - current accounting guidance.
     - regulatory guidance for appraisals and evaluations.
     - guidance in this booklet pertaining to the rental of residential OREO.
     - the Protecting Tenants at Foreclosure Act.
     - the Servicemembers Civil Relief Act.
     - risks posed by environmental contamination.
   - Determine if the bank's policies address risks associated with foreclosed properties as described in "Managing Foreclosed Properties" and appendix B, "Guidance on Potential Issues With Foreclosed Residential Properties as Servicer or Trustee."

2. Verify that the board of directors periodically reviews and approves the bank's OREO policies.

## Processes

Processes are the procedures, programs, and practices that impose order on a bank's pursuit of its objectives. Processes define how daily activities are carried out. Effective processes are consistent with the underlying policies and are governed by appropriate checks and balances (such as internal controls).

**Objective:** To determine whether the bank has adequate processes in place to execute its OREO policies and procedures.

1. Evaluate whether processes are effective, consistent with established policies and procedures, and effectively communicated to appropriate staff. Do they address

   - compliance with requirements of local authorities and prudent standards regarding property maintenance and security?
   - recording ownership interest in local land records?
   - OREO appraisal and accounting requirements?
   - payment of property insurance premiums and real estate taxes?
   - third-party relationships that include
     - written contracts outlining duties and obligations?
     - appropriate due-diligence of third parties?
     - ongoing oversight?
   - development and oversight of plans for the disposition of properties?
   - consideration of the Protecting Tenants at Foreclosure Act and the Servicemembers Civil Relief Act?
   - the establishment and governance of and accounting for SPEs that hold OREO, if applicable?

2. Determine whether the bank's processes include periodic reviews of OREO. Such reviews should address the following:

   - A valid appraisal or evaluation that supports the property's carrying value. This review should be completed at least annually.
   - Marketing plans and documented sales efforts, including all external inquiries and offers.
   - The prudence and proper authorization of additional expenditures on the property.
   - Changes in tax status, zoning restrictions, other liens, etc.
   - Compliance with accounting requirements.
   - Reporting of acquisitions and disposal of OREO assets to the board or its designated committee.

3. Before foreclosure, do procedures require to the extent possible

   - the evaluation of property for the presence of contaminants, including
     - lead-based paint in residential housing constructed before 1978?
     - underground or aboveground storage tanks?
     - asbestos?
     - groundwater contamination?
     - other known contaminants used in or produced by activities consistent with the historic use of the property?
     - other known contaminants common to the area?
   - an evaluation of the risks of foreclosing on contaminated property?

- formulation and implementation of appropriate plans to manage contaminants and mitigate the liability the contamination may impose?

4. Assess the adequacy of the bank's processes for the acquisition, holding or disposition of the following types of OREO:

**Former Banking Premises**

- Was the property transferred to OREO when it ceased to be used as banking premises?
- If operations were relocated, was the property transferred to OREO upon relocation from the former banking premises to the new banking premises?

**Real Estate Held for Future Expansion**

- Within one year of acquisition, did the board or a delegated committee approve a resolution for use of the property?
- Will the bank use the property within five years?

**Real Estate Held Under a Capital or Operating Lease**

To determine if the bank has disposed of its interest, consider whether

- the bank has assigned the lease to another party.
- if the bank has not assigned the lease, it has sublet the premises to another party and whether the remaining term of the sublease matches the remaining term of the original lease entered into by the bank (i.e., is it coterminous?).

5. Review the bank's disposition processes. Consider whether

- the bank's efforts to dispose of OREO are diligent and ongoing.
- the bank maintains adequate documentation of its marketing and sales efforts.
- the bank maintains acceptable documentation to support asking prices.
- the bank maintains acceptable documentation to justify the acceptance of lower bids.
- management has requested or received OCC permission to hold OREO for more than five years, if applicable.

6. For OREO sales that did not qualify for sales treatment according to GAAP, determine whether the bank continues to report the properties as OREO.

# Personnel

Personnel are the bank staff and managers who execute or oversee processes. Personnel should be qualified and competent, and should perform appropriately. They should understand the bank's mission, values, principles, policies, and processes. Banks should design compensation programs to attract, develop, and retain qualified personnel. In addition, compensation programs should be structured in a manner that encourages strong risk management practices.

**Objective:** To determine management's ability to supervise OREO in a safe and sound manner.

1. Given the scope and complexity of the bank's OREO, assess the management structure and staffing. Consider

   - the adequacy of staffing and volume of staff turnover.
   - the use of outsourcing arrangements for functions such as property management and marketing.
   - whether reporting lines encourage open communication and limit the chances of conflicts of interest.
   - the capability to address identified deficiencies.
   - responsiveness to regulatory, accounting, industry, and technological changes.

2. Given the scope and complexity of the bank's OREO activities, assess the experience, education and training, and demonstrated expertise and competency of management and staff. Consider

   - the suitability of an incumbent's experience and training for his or her position, particularly with respect to OREO property and accounting issues.
   - the availability, adequacy, and requirements for training to keep management and staff current with regulatory and other changes affecting the bank and its acquisition, management, and disposition of OREO.
   - the experience and training or education of individuals responsible for the bank's appraisal and evaluation program.

3. Evaluate the effectiveness of the bank's management of third-party relationships and whether they are subject to the same risk management process that would be expected if the bank were conducting the activities directly. Does the risk management process include

   - written contracts outlining the duties, obligations, and responsibilities of the parties involved?
   - appropriate due diligence before entering a third-party contract?
   - ongoing oversight of the third parties and third-party activities?

4. Assess performance management and compensation programs. Consider whether these programs measure and reward performance that aligns with the bank's strategic objectives and risk tolerance.

   If the bank offers incentive compensation programs, ensure that they are consistent with OCC Bulletin 2010-24, "Incentive Compensation: Interagency Guidance on Sound Incentive Compensation Policies," including compliance with its three key principles:

(1) provide employees with incentives that appropriately balance risk and reward; (2) be compatible with effective controls and risk management; and (3) be supported by strong corporate governance, including active and effective oversight by the bank's board of directors.

# Control Systems

Control systems are the functions (such as internal and external audits, risk review, and quality assurance) and information systems that bank managers use to measure performance, make decisions about risk, and assess the effectiveness of processes. Control functions should have clear reporting lines, adequate resources, and appropriate authority. Management information systems should provide timely, accurate, and relevant feedback.

**Objective:** To determine whether the bank has systems in place to provide accurate and timely assessments of the risks associated with its OREO activities.

1. Evaluate the effectiveness of monitoring systems intended to identify, measure, and track exceptions to policies and established limits. Do the systems permit the effective monitoring of exceptions to

   - regulatory and internally established limits on holding periods?
   - policies pertaining to OREO expenditures?
   - policies governing the appraisal or evaluation of OREO?
   - policies establishing standards for the management of OREO?
   - policies governing the disposition of OREO?

2. Determine whether management information systems provide timely, accurate, and useful information to evaluate risk levels and trends in the bank's OREO portfolio. Can the banks systems report

   - the amount, volume, and type of OREO?
   - aging of OREO?
   - sales data including prices, volume, marketing times, and disposition proceeds relative to book value?
   - OREO expenditures?

3. Determine whether the reports used to convey and monitor information are effectively utilized by management and staff. Consider

   - the data presented by the reports.
   - the accuracy of the data.
   - the timeliness and frequency of the reports.
   - who receives the reports.

- who is responsible for monitoring the data presented by the reports.
- how the data is used by the board, management, or staff.

4. In consultation with the examiner assigned responsibility for assessing the bank's overall audit program, assess the scope, frequency, effectiveness, and independence of the internal and external audits or other independent reviews of OREO. The audits or reviews should test for compliance with OREO statutes, regulations, and other guidance and compliance with the bank's policies and procedures. Consider

- the frequency and scope of audits and reviews.
- the qualifications of audit and review personnel.
- the comprehensiveness and accuracy of findings and recommendations.
- if violations or exceptions were noted, determine whether management took appropriate and timely corrective action(s).

5. Determine whether the bank's appraisal and evaluation review process provides adequate control to ensure that the appraisal and review function for OREO is effective and consistent with regulatory guidance and the bank's own policies and procedures.

# Conclusions

## Conclusion: The aggregate level of each associated risk is (low, moderate, or high).
## The direction of each associated risk is (increasing, stable, or decreasing).

**Objective:** To determine, document, and communicate overall findings and conclusions regarding the examination of OREO activities.

1. Discuss preliminary examination findings and conclusions with the EIC, including the

   - quantity of associated risks.
   - quality of risk management.
   - direction of risks associated with OREO.
   - overall risk in OREO activities.
   - violations of law and regulation and other concerns.

   In reaching conclusions about OREO risk management, consider

   - the adequacy of policies, processes, and controls.
   - how actual practices conform to established policies and processes.
   - adverse trends.
   - significant internal control deficiencies.
   - any recommended corrective actions needed to correct deficiencies.
   - the quality of departmental management.
   - the adequacy of management information systems and reporting.
   - the adequacy of internal and external audits.
   - other matters of significance.

2. If substantive safety and soundness concerns remain unresolved that may have a material adverse effect on the bank, expand the scope of the examination by completing verification procedures.

3. In consultation with the EIC, discuss examination findings with bank management, including violations, recommendations, and conclusions about risks and risk management practices. If necessary, obtain commitments for corrective action.

4. Compose conclusion comments, highlighting any issues that should be included in the ROE. Address the

   - adequacy of policies and procedures for the acquisition, holding, and disposition of OREO.
   - amount, volume, type, and trend of OREO.

- volume, type, and trend of OREO dispositions.
- volume of OREO expenditures if significant.
- property sample results including valuation, accounting, management, marketing efforts and compliance with OREO policy including expenditures and their justification.
- violations of law and regulation.
- quality of board oversight and supervision.
- quality of staffing.
- accuracy and timeliness of management information systems (MIS).
- effectiveness of OREO administration and internal controls.
- effectiveness of the bank's appraisal and evaluation program and the reliability of valuations.
- extent to which OREO activities and risk management practices affect inter-related risks including liquidity, price, operational, compliance, and reputation risks.
- compliance with applicable laws, rules, and regulations.
- recommended corrective actions and management's commitment to implement, if necessary.

5. Complete the following table summarizing the risks associated with the bank's OREO activities.

| Summary of Risks Associated With OREO Activities | | | | |
|---|---|---|---|---|
| Risk category | Quantity of risk (Low, moderate, high) | Quality of risk management (Weak, satisfactory, strong) | Aggregate level of risk (Low, moderate, high) | Direction of risk (Increasing, stable, decreasing) |
| Liquidity | | | | |
| Price | | | | |
| Operational | | | | |
| Compliance | | | | |
| Reputation | | | | |

6. Determine, in consultation with the EIC, whether identified risks or other issues are significant enough to bring them to the board's attention in the ROE. If so, prepare comments to include in the "Matters Requiring Attention" section of the ROE.

7. Update the OCC's information system and any applicable ROE schedules or tables.

8. Write a memorandum specifically describing what the OCC should do in the future to effectively supervise OREO in the bank, including time frames, staffing, and workdays required.

9. Update, organize, and reference work papers in accordance with OCC policy.

10. Ensure any paper or electronic media that contain sensitive bank or customer information are properly disposed of or secured.

# Internal Control Questionnaire

An internal control questionnaire (ICQ) helps an examiner assess a bank's internal controls for an area. ICQs typically address standard controls that provide day-to-day protection of bank assets and financial records. The examiner decides the extent to which it is necessary to complete or update ICQs during examination planning or after reviewing the findings and conclusions of the core assessment.

1. Are the preparation, addition, and posting of subsidiary OREO records tested by persons who do not have direct physical or accounting control of those assets?

2. Are the subsidiary OREO records reconciled at least monthly to the appropriate general ledger accounts by persons who do not have direct physical or accounting control of those assets?

3. Are supporting documents maintained for all entries to OREO accounts?

4. Is revenue received from OREO accounted for as other noninterest income in the period it is received?

5. Are expenses for the maintenance of OREO, including taxes, accounted for as other noninterest expense in the period it is incurred?

6. Are acquisitions and disposals of OREO reported to the board of directors or its designated committee?

7. Does the bank maintain insurance coverage on OREO, including liability coverage when necessary?

8. Does the bank pay real estate taxes either as they are due or before they become a lien on the property?

9. Does the bank have an inspection program that permits it to maintain an assessment of the current condition of OREO?

10. Does the bank give proper notification to the borrower before foreclosure or repossession?

11. Does the bank record collateral property as OREO upon foreclosure regardless of any ensuing statutory redemption periods?

12. Does the bank hold valid title, or valid claim to title if bank has taken possession, to OREO?

13. Does the bank review all OREO it acquires by deed in lieu of foreclosure for prior liens?

14. Does the bank have valid appraisals or evaluations upon transfer to OREO?

15. Does the bank have valid appraisals or evaluations to support the sale of OREO?

16. Does the bank or its bonded agent directly control rental income received from OREO?

17. Do any unbonded agents collect rents or manage properties?

18. Does the bank document third-party activities performed on behalf of the bank?

19. Are all parcels of OREO reviewed periodically, consistent with the frequency established by the bank's policy, for

- a valid appraisal or evaluation?
- documented inquiries and offers?
- documented sales efforts?
- evidence of the prudence of and proper authorization of additional advances?
- marketing plans for disposal of the property?
- changes in tax status, zoning restrictions, other liens, etc.?

20. Are the bank's OREO policies and procedures in writing?

**Conclusion**

21. Is the foregoing information an adequate basis for evaluating internal control in that there are no significant additional internal auditing procedures, accounting controls, administrative controls, or other circumstances that impair any controls or mitigate any weaknesses indicated above? (Explain negative answers briefly, and indicate conclusions as to their effect on specific examination or verification procedures.)

22. Based on the answers to the foregoing questions, internal control for OREO activities is considered (strong, satisfactory, weak).

# Verification Procedures

Verification procedures are used to verify the existence of assets and liabilities or to test the reliability of financial records. Examiners generally do not perform verification procedures as part of an examination. Rather, verification procedures are performed when substantive safety and soundness concerns are identified that are not mitigated by the bank's risk management systems and internal controls.

1. Using appropriate sampling techniques, select specific properties and determine whether

   - the asset was recorded as OREO when the bank obtained title or possession, whichever occurred first.
   - legal fees and direct costs of acquiring title, including payment of existing liens, taxes, and recording fees, are expensed when incurred and not capitalized.
   - insurance, including liability coverage, is adequate, and the bank is named as insured (or as loss payee if the bank does not have title).

2. Using appropriate sampling techniques, select specific properties, and for expenses incurred in maintaining the properties or capitalized costs of improvement and development

   - trace transactions to any succeeding summary records and to postings in the general ledger.
   - determine whether the bank performed an inspection before disbursing funds for capital improvements or development and construction costs.

3. Trace proceeds received from the rental of OREO; determine whether the bank receives the proceeds directly and whether the amount received agrees with the stated terms of the rental contract.

4. Review sales proceeds that the bank receives from partial sales of OREO, such as lot sales or condominiums sales; determine whether the bank records the receipt of the proceeds, and records any gains or losses on the sale of OREO in accordance with GAAP.

# Appendixes

## Appendix A: Exchanging OREO for Interests in Other Assets

### Exchanging of Participation Interests in OREO by National Banks

In a limited number of circumstances, a national bank may acquire a non-controlling equity interest in a special purpose entity (SPE), such as a limited liability company (LLC), in exchange for its interest in OREO. The OCC has approved this type of exchange in which an LLC is established as a means for the participants in the original loan to hold the real estate collateral acquired through or in lieu of foreclosure. The participants in the original loan are the members of the LLC, and each participant holds an interest in the LLC equivalent to its participation interest in the loan and OREO. The LLC is established specifically to manage and dispose of the OREO. The member banks retain control over the OREO asset and maintain the same level of risk as before the exchange. The exchange, however, enables the participants to manage and dispose of the OREO more efficiently than if each bank had to manage its own partial interest in the property.

A national bank wishing to complete such an exchange of its loan interest for an equivalent SPE interest has two options. The bank may follow the well-established licensing procedures in 12 CFR 5.36 for making a non-controlling investment by submitting a notice (an option limited to well-capitalized, well-managed banks) or an application, as appropriate. Alternatively, the bank may seek approval from its supervisory office (SO) under the standards established in OCC Interpretive Letter No. 1123. SO approval under the standards established in Interpretive Letter No. 1123 is available only for those instances, as described previously, in which the participants in a loan form an SPE to hold, manage, and dispose of the OREO collateral acquired for debts previously contracted. Interpretive Letter No. 1123 does not provide legal support for national banks to exchange OREO for equity interest in an entity aggregating various unrelated OREO parcels from multiple banks.

## OCC Interpretive Letter No. 1123

The interpretive letter[12] describes a procedure under which a national bank could seek non-objection from its SO to exchange a participation interest in OREO for an interest in an LLC that would manage, market, and sell the OREO. Provided the bank makes certain representations concerning the exchange, the SO can give the bank a written notification of non-objection to the exchange. The bank must receive the SO's non-objection before making the exchange.

Before the SO may provide a non-objection notification, the bank is required to make certain representations that include the following:

---

[12] OCC Interpretive Letter No. 1123, " Re: Exchange of interest in real property acquired DPC for interest in an entity which would dispose of the real property" (September 18, 2009).

1. The bank's board of directors has determined that the exchange is in the best interests of the bank and would improve the ability of the bank to recover, or otherwise limit, its loan loss, and the basis for such determination has been documented.

2. The bank has adequate risk management and measurement systems and controls in place to enable it to exchange for, hold, and dispose of the LLC interest in a safe and sound manner.

3. The bank will not exchange the LLC interest for an interest in any other real or personal property.

4. The bank will ensure that the LLC complies with the provisions of the OCC's OREO regulation, 12 CFR Part 34, subpart E, including the appraisal requirements for OREO.

5. The bank will dispose of its interest in the LLC no later than five years from the date it initially acquired title to the OREO (unless granted an extension by the OCC as allowed by 12 USC 29).

## Supervisory Office Review and Non-Objection Notification

When a bank submits a request to its SO to make an exchange of an interest in OREO for an interest in an SPE which would hold the OREO, the SO will take the following steps.

- *Review the request, including the representations made by the bank and the basis for the representations.*

The SO should review the incoming request. The review should include an evaluation of the representations made by the bank and an analysis of the reasonableness of the support for the transaction. If the SO is not comfortable with the support given, it should request additional information from the bank to more fully assess the bank's representations.

For example, if the bank states that it has adequate risk management and measurement systems and controls to engage in the exchange in a safe and sound manner, the SO should ask the bank to provide an explanation of the systems and controls. If the bank states that it will ensure that the SPE complies with the provisions of the OCC's OREO regulation, the SO should ask the bank to describe the authority it has over the SPE and ensure compliance with the OREO regulation. The SO should request, in each instance, that the bank provide a copy of the SPE agreement or the relevant excerpts from the SPE agreement, to assess the basis for the bank's representations. The SO should contact District Counsel with any questions related to the SPE agreement or sufficiency of the representations.

- *Determine whether the bank's representations are sufficient or whether additional representations are necessary.*

To address safety and soundness concerns, the SO may request that the bank make additional representations. The five representations listed above are the minimum required for supervisory non-objection. The SO may require the bank to make any additional representations that the SO believes would be appropriate given the nature and character of the proposed exchange.

For example, the SO may wish to supervise and examine the activities of the SPE. In such an instance, the SO should require the bank to represent that the SPE would be subject to OCC supervision and examination and ensure that the SPE itself has agreed to be supervised and examined by the OCC. Such agreement is usually reflected in the SPE agreement.

- *Decide whether to issue a supervisory non-objection notification.*

If the SO is satisfied that the bank has made the necessary representations and that there is sufficient support for the representations, the SO may issue a written non-objection to the bank's proposed exchange. Such non-objection should make reference to (or could even recite) the representations made by the bank. For example, the notification letter may state that, based on the representations made by the bank, the SO poses no objection to the bank's proposal to exchange their participation interest in OREO for interest in an entity which would market and dispose of the OREO.

If the SO is not comfortable issuing a supervisory non-objection to a request pursuant to Interpretive Letter No. 1123, the SO should contact the District Licensing division of the OCC's Chief Counsel's office regarding the bank's ability to follow the well-established licensing procedures in 12 CFR 5.36 for making a noncontrolling investment. The notice process in 12 CFR 5.36(g)(1) is available to well-capitalized and well-managed banks and requires that the banks make certain representations and certifications, including that the activities of the SPE are conducted consistent with OCC policy and guidance. The 12 CFR 5.36 application process requires banks to make additional representations and certifications, including that the SPE agrees to be subject to OCC supervision and examination.

Examiners should work with the district office of the Chief Counsel's office to assist on issues with respect to the SPE agreements and representations.

## Exchanging OREO Interests for Other Assets

**The following guidance applies to national banks and FSAs.** Certain third-party companies market OREO exchange programs to banks as a purported means to reduce problem assets by exchanging OREO for an interest in another asset that is represented to be performing. This "performing asset" is often an equity interest in the entity acquiring the OREO or a trade for a large volume of loans, such as home equity lines of credit. These programs can raise significant safety and soundness, legal, and accounting concerns, and the OCC strongly encourages banks to consult with their SO before entering into any such agreements.

Common issues associated with the exchange of OREO assets for an equity interest (generally in a LLC) include

- the loss of control over OREO assets.
- the exchange of OREO for an asset of questionable liquidity and value.
- the commingling of OREO with real estate assets that may be of poorer quality.
- significant up-front and recurring management fees paid to the organizing company.
- unfavorable priority of payments between the bank and equity investors.

In addition, the entity acquiring the OREO may be involved in activities that are not permissible for banks, making the asset acquired by the bank impermissible. Moreover, the structure of the exchange transaction typically does not meet the accounting definition of a true sale. Thus, rather than improving its position, the bank ends up in an economically inferior situation, with additional legal and accounting issues.

Another example of transactions offered to banks to reduce their nonperforming asset balances is an "adjusted price trade." This type of transaction involves an offer to purchase the bank's nonperforming real estate loans or OREO at book value, with the stipulation that the bank purchase other assets, at inflated values, from the same party. An adjusted price trade is not only unsafe and unsound but may constitute fraud if it results in the misrepresentation of the bank's financial statements. Banks need to use caution when looking at novel methods of trading nonperforming OREO for other assets. Before entering into any type of OREO exchange, the bank should have a detailed, documented plan. At a minimum, bank management and the board of directors should

- document how the exchange is permissible and in the best interest of the bank, and how it would improve the bank's ability to recover or limit its loan loss. This determination should address how the transaction aligns with board-established strategies to reduce nonperforming assets. The board of directors should review the determination before approving the transaction.
- determine whether the exchange qualifies as a sale under ASC 860, "Transfers and Servicing." Policies and procedures should be in place to ensure that the bank is following GAAP, and the accounting policies and procedures should also address how to value and account for expenses related to the OREO and the exchanged asset at the consummation of the transaction and on an ongoing basis.
- identify the factors preventing the bank from selling the OREO and provide documentation supporting why the exchange will make the real estate more marketable.
- ensure that an accurate value of the exchanged asset is established, and determine a schedule or trigger points for when to update the value.
- ensure that adequate risk management, measurement systems, and controls are in place to enable the bank to exchange for, hold, and dispose of the acquired interest in a safe and sound manner.
- set parameters and methods for tracking assets received in the OREO exchange to avoid multiple exchanges for interests in any other real or personal property.
- ensure that any entity in which the bank acquires an interest complies with guidance governing OREO, including requirements for additional expenditures and appraisals or evaluations.
- conduct due diligence to determine and document that all activities are permissible banking activities. The activities to be performed by any entity in which the bank

acquires an interest in exchange for the OREO should be clearly documented, and the bank should obtain a commitment from the third party regarding activities performed.

- have processes in place for disposing of its interest in any such entity that are consistent with prescribed OREO holding periods.

# Appendix B: Guidance on Potential Issues With Foreclosed Residential Properties as Servicer or Trustee

This appendix highlights legal, safety and soundness, and community impact considerations of foreclosed properties as a servicer or trustee. Although the primary focus is residential, many of the same principles apply to commercial properties.

A bank's obligations with respect to foreclosed residential properties may differ depending upon the bank's role in the foreclosure—as owner of the foreclosed property, servicer or property manager, or securitization trustee—and the contractual agreements under which it operates. Understanding the requirements Fannie Mae and Freddie Mac or HUD impose on servicers is particularly crucial given the current role of these entities in the mortgage market.

## Considerations

As a matter of safe and sound banking practices, banks should have robust policies and procedures in place to address risks associated with foreclosed (or soon to be foreclosed) properties as servicer. Acquiring title to properties through foreclosure—either for the bank or as servicer for another mortgagee—results in new or expanded risks, including operating risk (which may include market valuation issues), compliance risk, and reputation risk. The bank should be sure it has identified all the risks and has policies and procedures for monitoring and controlling these risks. In establishing and implementing the policies and procedures, bank management and the board of directors should consider, at a minimum, the following obligations and risks:

### Obligations and Actions

Fannie Mae and Freddie Mac each have detailed guides setting forth servicer obligations and responsibilities for foreclosed properties and vacant properties in the process of foreclosure. In the case of private securitizations, the obligations are detailed in a document often called a pooling and servicing agreement (PSA).

- Servicers of foreclosed properties may be required to undertake many of the responsibilities of an owner, including providing maintenance and security, paying expenses, serving as the landlord for rentals, and marketing the property.
  - Servicers may be required to advance funds for taxes, insurance, and homeowners' association dues, as well as for maintenance and security expenses, some or all of which may be reimbursable.
  - Although rehabilitation, maintenance, and marketing of foreclosed properties acquired on behalf of Fannie Mae and Freddie Mac are typically handled by Fannie Mae and Freddie Mac, servicers may be required to perform routine upkeep—including winterization, as needed—until the property is assigned by Fannie Mae and Freddie Mac to a property manager.

- Servicers should ensure they follow Fannie Mae and Freddie Mac's applicable requirements or PSA requirements and guidelines for performing necessary maintenance and upkeep on the property.
  - The bank should maintain appropriate insurance on the property.
  - Servicers may be required to file claims with any mortgage insurers.
  - Some localities may require registration of foreclosed properties, properties in foreclosure, or vacant properties. Under the PSA or the Fannie Mae and Freddie Mac servicing guidelines, this requirement may be the responsibility of the servicer. Servicers should communicate with localities about other specific requirements with respect to foreclosed residential properties.
  - When disposing of foreclosed properties, servicers should look to the PSA or other servicing documents for specific requirements and responsibilities. Servicers may have responsibilities, as described above, under the Protecting Tenants at Foreclosure Act or applicable state law requirements that provide protections to tenants from eviction as a result of foreclosure on the property they are renting.

## Additional Issues as Servicer

- A bank acting as a servicer should have sufficient staffing and appropriate third-party vendor oversight to manage the portfolios of foreclosed properties.
- Rehabilitation or improvement of foreclosed properties should comply with local building codes, licensing requirements, and any requirements specified in servicing agreements.
- When disposing of foreclosed residential properties, banks acting as servicers should consider
  - contractual requirements for valuing and marketing the properties and addressing defects found at inspection. The servicer may be required to advance funds for these activities, though these funds may be recovered.
  - that disposition practices may carry reputation and litigation risks. Even when the servicer follows the disposition requirements in the servicing agreements, the impact of the dispositions reflects on the servicer and could result in reputation risk and risk of litigation.
  - opportunities to participate in and coordinate with state and local land bank programs, neighborhood stabilization programs, redevelopment programs, and other anti-blight programs, consistent with servicing agreements.

## Bank as Trustee of Securitization Trust Holding Title to Foreclosed Property

The securitization trustee is primarily responsible for (1) holding a lien on trust assets for the benefit of investors who purchase securities issued pursuant to the securitization and (2) administering the trust in conformance with requisite agreements. The trustee's duties and responsibilities are established by a PSA, trust agreement, or indenture. These agreements direct a securitization trustee to perform various complex ministerial functions. Such functions may include ensuring the timely receipt of payments from the servicer, calculating payments, remitting payments to investors, circulating information to investors, monitoring compliance, and determining if an event of default is triggered.

As permitted by the PSA, the trustee should work with the servicer to ensure the performance of the servicer's responsibilities. The securitization agreements may require a trustee to appoint a successor servicer or to take over servicing in the event the original servicer fails to perform its duties or defaults. These agreements generally do not grant the trustee any powers or duties with respect to the foreclosure or the maintenance, sale, or disposition of foreclosed properties. Instead, these responsibilities typically reside with the servicer.

Nevertheless, a bank trustee should be aware of potential reputation and litigation risks when a servicer undertakes foreclosure actions in the trustee's name as the secured party. Additionally, if the securitization agreements require a bank trustee to act as a replacement servicer until a successor servicer is appointed, the bank trustee will also be exposed to credit risk.

# References

## Laws

12 USC 29, "Power to hold real property" (national banks)
12 USC 161, "Reports to Comptroller of the Currency"
Public Law 111-22, "Helping Families Save Their Homes Act of 2009," Title VII, sections 701-704, "Protecting Tenants at Foreclosure Act," as amended by the Dodd–Frank Wall Street Reform and Consumer Protection Act, section 1484
50 USC appendix, sections 501-597b, "Servicemembers Civil Relief Act"

## Regulations

12 CFR 32, "Lending Limits" (national banks and FSAs)
12 CFR 34, subparts C—"Appraisals" and E—"Other Real Estate Owned" (national banks)
12 CFR 34, subpart D, appendix A (national banks) and appendix to 12 CFR 160.101 (FSAs), "Interagency Guidelines for Real Estate Lending"
12 CFR 160.30, "General Lending and Investment Powers" (FSAs)
12 CFR 160.160, "Asset Classification" (FSAs)
12 CFR 160.172, "Reevaluation of Real Estate Owned" (FSAs)
12 CFR 164, "Appraisals" (FSAs)
12 CFR 167.1, "Definitions—Equity Investments in Real Property" (FSAs)
12 CFR 167.5, "Components of Capital" (FSAs)

## Comptroller's Handbook

### Examination Process
"Bank Supervision Process"
"Community Bank Supervision"
"Federal Branches and Agencies Supervision"
"Large Bank Supervision"

### Safety and Soundness, "Asset Quality"
"Commercial Real Estate Lending"
"Concentrations of Credit"
"Installment Loans"
"Loan Portfolio Management"
"Mortgage Banking"
"Residential Real Estate Lending"

### Consumer Compliance
"Protecting Tenants at Foreclosure Act"
"Servicemembers Civil Relief Act"

# OCC Issuances

*Bank Accounting Advisory Series*

OCC Bulletin 2001-47, "Third-Party Relationships: Risk Management Principles" (November 1, 2001)

OCC Bulletin 2004-25, "Classification of Securities: Uniform Agreement on the Classification of Securities" (June 15, 2004)

OCC Bulletin 2006-46, "Concentrations in Commercial Real Estate Lending, Sound Risk Management Practices: Interagency Guidance on CRE Concentration Risk Management" (December 6, 2006)

OCC Bulletin 2010-24, "Incentive Compensation: Interagency Guidance on Sound Incentive Compensation Policies" (June 30, 2010)

OCC Bulletin 2010-42, "Sound Practices for Appraisals and Evaluations: Interagency Appraisal and Evaluation Guidelines" (December 10, 2010)

OCC Bulletin 2011-29, "Foreclosure Management: Supervisory Guidance" (June 20, 2011)

OCC Interpretive Letter No. 1123, "Re: Exchange of interest in real property acquired DPC for interest in an entity which would dispose of the real property" (September 18, 2009)

# Other

**Accounting Standards Codification**

ASC 310, "Receivables"

ASC 360-20, "Real Estate Sales"

ASC 820-10, "Fair Value Measurement"

ASC 835-20, "Capitalization of Interest"

ASC 860, "Transfers and Servicing"

ASC 970-340, "Real Estate—Other Assets and Deferred Costs"

www.ingramcontent.com/pod-product-compliance
Lightning Source LLC
Chambersburg PA
CBHW080616290526
45790CB00007B/2796